write

need

ride

talk

feed

teach

The Daddy Book

Published by Silver Press,
A Division of Simon & Schuster
299 Jefferson Road, Parsippany, New Jersey 07054

Designed by Studio Goodwin Sturges

Manufactured in the United States of America
10 9 8 7 6 5 4 3 2 1

Library of Congress Cataloging-in-Publication Data

Morris, Ann, 1930-
The daddy book/by Ann Morris: photographs by Ken Heyman.
p. cm.—(The World's Family series)
Summary: A loving, positive look at fathers around the world and
how they relate to their children.
1. Father and child—Juvenile literature.   2. Fathers—Juvenile literature.
[1. Father and child.   2. Fathers.] I. Heyman, Ken, ill. II. Title. III.
Series.
HQ755.85.N67 1996
306.874'2—dc20 95-14491 CIP AC
ISBN 0-382-24695-0 (JHC)   ISBN 0-382-24696-9 (LSB)
ISBN 0-382-24697-7 (PBK)

The Daddy Book

By Ann Morris
Photographs by Ken Heyman

Silver Press
Parsippany, New Jersey

This is my daddy.

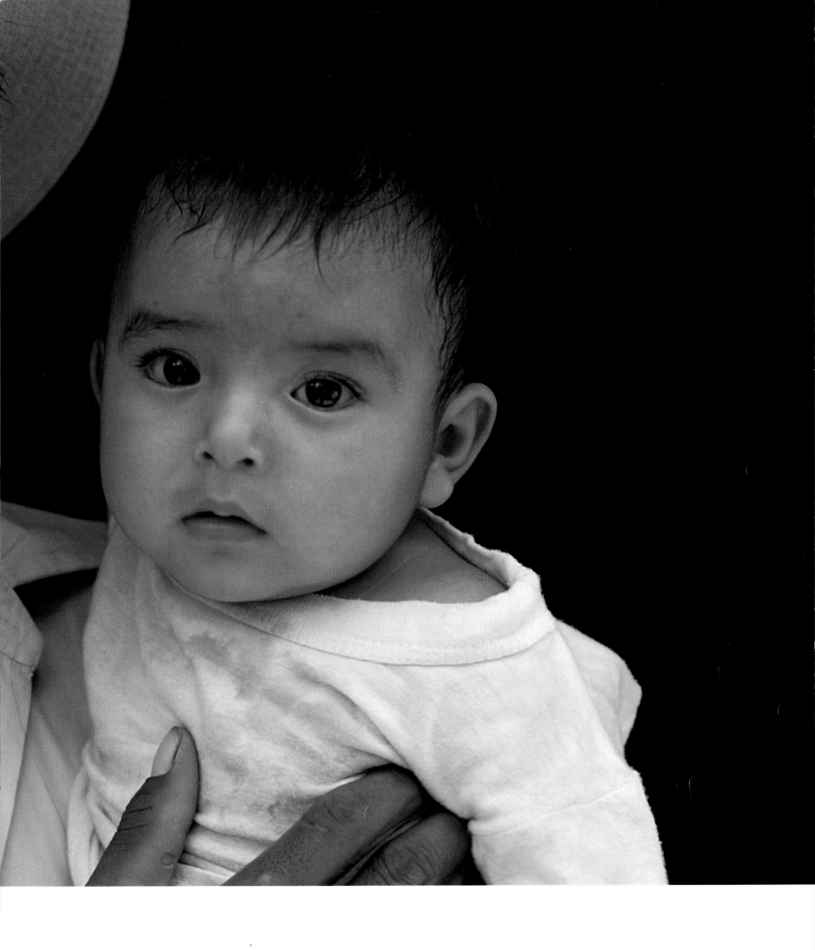

And this is my daddy.

And this is my daddy.

We're all part of a family.

Daddies love you in many ways.

They tell you stories.

They play songs for you.

They take you fishing

and teach you many things . . . to read,

to write,

to ride a bike,

and to feed chickens.

Daddies play with their children

and talk with them about many things.

Daddies have daddies, too.

Sometimes they are called "Grandpa" or
"Gramps." We call ours "Opa."

Daddies help you feel good.

Wherever you are
and whatever you do,

daddies are there for you
when you need them!

Index to Daddies

Page 18: Timothy, who can't see, likes to go very fast with his father on the back of a bicycle built for two.

Page 19: In Arizona this Pueblo boy and his dad feed the chickens every day.

 **Page 20:** Father and daughter enjoy rough-housing in this New York City apartment on a rainy Sunday.

 **Page 22:** This father in Cairo, Egypt, buys and sells camels. Father and son are waiting for customers in the camel market.

Page 24: In Switzer-land, where the winters are very cold, most everyone wears a hat.

Page 25: Grandpa is visiting from Germany. His grandchildren call him Opa, which means "grandpa" in German.

 **Page 26:** This father is a taxi driver from Taiwan. His son is very excited when his dad stops by school to see him.

 **Page 28:** When this little girl is sad, her daddy is there to comfort her.

Page 29: At this Apache powwow, this dad is wearing a headdress of eagle feathers. A powwow may be a social event.

Ann Morris

Ann Morris's many books for children include **Bread Bread Bread, Hats Hats Hats, How Teddy Bears Are Made** and **Dancing to America**. She has been a teacher in public and private schools and has taught courses in language arts, children's literature, and writing for children at Bank Street College, Teachers College, Queens College of the City University of New York, and at The New School in New York City.

Ken Heyman

Ken Heyman's photographic career has taken him into the heart of many indigenous cultures. His photographs have appeared in publications such as **Life, Look,** and **The New York Times**, and his work has been exhibited on three continents. His photographs illustrate numerous children's books, and he is the co-author of **Family** with Margaret Mead. He lives in New York City.